# THE ART OF SONGWRITING

## TECHNIQUES AND STRATEGIES FOR CREATING HIT SONGS

# INTRODUCTION

The music industry is a highly competitive field, and success often depends on the ability to craft songs that connect with listeners on an emotional level. Songwriting is a critical component of this process, and the art of creating lyrics and melodies that resonate with an audience is a skill that requires both creativity and technique. In "The Art of Songwriting: Techniques and Strategies for Creating Hit Songs," we explore the craft of songwriting in-depth, providing aspiring songwriters with the tools they need to write music that not only entertains but also resonates with listeners. From analyzing popular songs to learning the basics of melody and harmony, this book offers a comprehensive guide to the art of songwriting, providing readers with the knowledge and confidence to create music that speaks to the hearts and minds of audiences around the world. Whether you are an aspiring songwriter or an experienced musician looking to take your craft to the next level, "The Art of Songwriting" is the ultimate guide to creating hit songs that stand the test of time.

# CONTENT

# CHAPTER 1

# THE SIGNIFICANCE OF SONGWRITING IN THE MUSIC INDUSTRY

Songwriting is an art form that has played a critical role in the music industry since the dawn of time. It is an essential component that forms the backbone of every musical production, and it is the creative process of crafting lyrics and melodies that resonate with an audience and convey a message or emotion.

The art of songwriting is a creative process that allows a writer to express themselves through words and music. It can take various forms and styles, from ballads to rock songs, pop, country, and more. Regardless of the genre, songwriting is a craft that requires a great deal of creativity, skill, and dedication.

Songwriting plays a crucial role in the success of a musical piece. It is often considered the most important factor in determining the commercial viability of a song. The quality of the lyrics and the melody can make or break a song's success, and therefore, the role of the songwriter is critical in the music industry.

At its core, songwriting is about telling stories and conveying emotions. It is about connecting with people on a deeper level and capturing the essence of the human experience in a way that resonates with the listener. Songwriters must find a way to express their thoughts and feelings through their music in a way that speaks to others.

Songwriting is a collaborative process that involves many people in the music industry, including performers, producers, and engineers. A successful songwriter must work closely with these individuals to create a cohesive musical composition that resonates with the audience.

The music industry is highly competitive, and the demand for quality songwriting has never been higher. To succeed as a songwriter, one must possess a unique style and voice that sets them apart from the rest. A great songwriter must have an innate ability to connect with people on an emotional level, and they must be able to communicate their ideas effectively.

The significance of songwriting in the music industry is evident by the number of awards and recognition given to songwriters. The Grammy Awards, for instance, recognizes excellence in songwriting with categories such as Song of the Year and Best Song Written for Visual Media. The Songwriters Hall of Fame is another institution that recognizes the significant contributions of songwriters to the music industry.

Songwriting is a craft that requires constant refinement, and even the most successful songwriters must continue to hone their skills. The ability to create music that connects with people on an emotional level is a gift that few possess, and it is a talent that must be cultivated and nurtured over time.

In conclusion, songwriting is a crucial aspect of the music industry that plays a significant role in the success of any musical piece. Songwriters are responsible for creating the foundation upon which performers and producers build their music, and their contributions are essential to the industry's growth and success. It is an art form that requires creativity, skill, and dedication, and it is a craft that will continue to shape the music industry for years to come.

# THE DIFFERENCES BETWEEN SONGWRITING AND OTHER MUSICAL SKILLS

Songwriting is a highly specialized skill within the music industry, and it differs significantly from other musical skills such as performance or production. While performance and production involve the execution and presentation of music, songwriting involves the creation of original lyrics and melodies. In this section, we will explore the differences between songwriting and other musical skills, and why each is essential to the music industry.

Performance is one of the most visible aspects of the music industry, and it involves the interpretation and execution of music in a live or recorded setting. Performers must have a deep understanding of the musical structure, rhythm, and melody of a song, as well as the ability to convey emotion through their performance. While performance skills are essential to the success of a song, they do not involve the creative process of writing the music.

Production, on the other hand, involves the technical aspects of music creation, such as recording, mixing, and mastering. Producers must have an in-depth understanding of music technology, including software and hardware, as well as the ability to work with musicians and performers to create a cohesive musical product. While production skills are essential to the success of a song, they do not involve the creative process of writing the music.

Songwriting, on the other hand, involves the creative process of composing original lyrics and melodies. It is the art of crafting a song from scratch, from the initial concept to the finished product. Songwriters must have a deep understanding of the music they are creating, including the structure, rhythm, melody, and harmony of the song. They must also have the ability to express themselves through their lyrics and connect with their audience on an emotional level.

One of the key differences between songwriting and other musical skills is that songwriting involves a significant amount of creative thinking and imagination. While performance and production require technical skills, songwriting requires a level of artistic talent and intuition. Songwriters must be able to draw on their experiences and emotions to create music that resonates with their audience.

Another difference between songwriting and other musical skills is that songwriting is often a solitary activity. While performance and production typically involve collaboration with others, songwriting is often a personal endeavor. Songwriters must be able to work independently, generating ideas and concepts on their own.

The significance of songwriting in the music industry is evident by the number of awards and recognition given to songwriters. Songwriters are responsible for creating original compositions that are not only melodically and lyrically engaging but also have the potential to connect with the listener on a deeper emotional level. They are often the unsung heroes of the music industry, creating the foundations upon which performers and producers build their music.

In conclusion, songwriting is a highly specialized skill within the music industry that differs significantly from other musical skills such as performance and production. While performance and production involve the execution and presentation of music, songwriting involves the creative process of composing original lyrics and melodies. Songwriting requires a significant amount of creativity and imagination, and it is often a solitary activity. Despite the differences between songwriting and other musical skills, each is essential to the success of a song, and the music industry as a whole.

# THE CHALLENGES AND REWARDS OF SUCCESSFUL SONGWRITING

Songwriting is a challenging but rewarding pursuit for musicians and artists who are passionate about creating original music. Writing hit songs that resonate with listeners and stand the test of time is no easy feat. It takes time, effort, and dedication to hone the skills needed to create music that captivates an audience. In this section, we will explore the challenges and rewards of successful songwriting.

One of the biggest challenges of successful songwriting is finding inspiration. Songwriters must be able to tap into their creativity and draw from their personal experiences and emotions to create music that is authentic and relatable. However, inspiration is not always easy to come by, and songwriters may experience writer's block or struggle to find the right words or melody.

Another challenge of successful songwriting is the competition. The music industry is highly competitive, and there are countless talented songwriters vying for attention. Songwriters must be able to create music that stands out from the crowd and captures the attention of listeners. They must also be able to adapt to changing trends and genres in music and stay relevant in an ever-evolving industry.

Writing hit songs also requires a significant amount of time and effort. Songwriters must be willing to put in long hours crafting lyrics and melodies, experimenting with different chord progressions, and perfecting their sound. They must be able to handle constructive criticism and use feedback to improve their work.

Despite the challenges of successful songwriting, the rewards can be significant. One of the most rewarding aspects of successful songwriting is the ability to connect with an audience. Music has the power to evoke strong emotions and memories, and successful songwriters are able to create music that resonates with their listeners on a deep level. There is no greater feeling than hearing someone sing along to a song you have written or seeing the impact your music has on someone's life.

Successful songwriting can also lead to financial rewards. Hit songs can generate significant royalties and income from licensing and performances. Songwriters who achieve success can also enjoy increased exposure and opportunities in the music industry, including collaborations with other artists and the chance to write for major films, television shows, and advertising campaigns.

In conclusion, successful songwriting is a challenging but rewarding pursuit for musicians and artists. It requires creativity, dedication, and the ability to connect with an audience on an emotional level. While the challenges of finding inspiration, facing competition, and putting in long hours can be daunting, the rewards of connecting with listeners and achieving financial success make it all worth it. For those who are passionate about music and willing to put in the work, successful songwriting can be a fulfilling and lucrative career path.

# CHAPTER 2
## ELEMENTS OF SONGWRITING

## A REVIEW OF THE BASIC ELEMENTS OF SONGWRITING

Songwriting is a complex art form that requires a mastery of several basic elements. In this section, we will review the key components of songwriting, including melody, harmony, rhythm, and lyrics.

Melody is the most recognizable and memorable aspect of a song. It is the main tune that is sung or played by the vocals or instruments. The melody should be catchy, memorable, and easy to sing along to. It should also fit the mood and lyrics of the song. Songwriters use different techniques to create a melody, such as using repetition, variation, and contrast.

Harmony refers to the chords and harmonies that support the melody. It creates a sense of depth and richness to the overall sound of the song. Harmony can be simple or complex, depending on the songwriter's preference. It can also change throughout the song to create different moods or emphasize certain lyrics or melodies.

Rhythm is the driving force of a song. It provides the underlying beat and tempo that supports the melody and lyrics. A well-crafted rhythm can make a song feel more energetic, emotional, or playful. Songwriters can use different rhythmic patterns and variations to create interest and variation in the song.

Lyrics are the words that accompany the melody. They tell a story, express an emotion, or convey a message. The lyrics should be clear, concise, and easy to understand. They should also be relatable and resonate with the audience. Songwriters can use different techniques to create lyrics, such as using metaphors, similes, and wordplay.

In addition to these basic elements, there are other factors that songwriters consider when writing a song. These can include dynamics, instrumentation, arrangement, and production. Dynamics refer to the changes in volume and intensity throughout the song, while instrumentation refers to the instruments used to create the music. Arrangement refers to how the different elements of the song are organized, and production refers to the overall sound quality of the recording.

In conclusion, songwriting involves several key elements that must be carefully crafted to create a successful song. Melody, harmony, rhythm, and lyrics are the most important components of a song, but other factors such as dynamics, instrumentation, arrangement, and production can also play a significant role. By mastering these basic elements and using them to create a cohesive and compelling piece of music, songwriters can achieve success and connect with audiences on a deeper level.

# THE IMPORTANCE OF EACH ELEMENT IN CREATING SUCCESSFUL SONGS

Each element of songwriting plays an important role in creating successful songs. In this section, we will explore the significance of each element and how they work together to create a cohesive and compelling piece of music.

Melody is perhaps the most important element of songwriting, as it is the main tune that listeners will remember and sing along to. A strong melody should be catchy, memorable, and easy to sing along to. It should also fit the mood and lyrics of the song. A great melody can make a song stand out and create an emotional connection with listeners.

Harmony is also crucial in creating successful songs, as it provides the underlying chords and harmonies that support the melody. The right harmony can create a sense of depth and richness to the overall sound of the song. Harmony can be simple or complex, and it can change throughout the song to create different moods or emphasize certain lyrics or melodies.

Rhythm is another essential element of songwriting, as it provides the beat and tempo that supports the melody and lyrics. A well-crafted rhythm can make a song feel more energetic, emotional, or playful. It can also help to create interest and variation in the song by using different rhythmic patterns and variations.

Lyrics are also critical in creating successful songs, as they tell a story, express an emotion, or convey a message. Great lyrics should be clear, concise, and easy to understand. They should also be relatable and resonate with the audience. Well-crafted lyrics can make a song more memorable and help to create an emotional connection with listeners.

Other elements of songwriting, such as dynamics, instrumentation, arrangement, and production, can also play significant roles in creating successful songs. Dynamics refer to the changes in volume and intensity throughout the song, while instrumentation refers to the instruments used to create the music. Arrangement refers to how the different elements of the song are organized, and production refers to the overall sound quality of the recording.

In conclusion, each element of songwriting plays an important role in creating successful songs. Melody, harmony, rhythm, and lyrics are the most important components of a song, but other factors such as dynamics, instrumentation, arrangement, and production can also play a significant role. By mastering each element and using them to create a cohesive and compelling piece of music, songwriters can achieve success and connect with audiences on a deeper level.

# TECHNIQUES FOR INCORPORATING THESE ELEMENTS INTO SONGWRITING

Incorporating the key elements of songwriting into a cohesive and compelling piece of music requires skill and practice. In this section, we will explore some techniques that can help songwriters incorporate melody, harmony, rhythm, and lyrics into their songwriting process.

Start with a strong melody: Begin by creating a memorable and catchy melody that fits the mood and lyrics of the song. Experiment with different notes, rhythms, and variations to create a melody that stands out and is easy to sing along to.

Build a harmonic foundation: Once you have a melody, add chords and harmonies that support and enhance it. Experiment with different chord progressions and harmonic structures to create a sense of depth and richness to the overall sound of the song.

Focus on rhythm: Develop a strong rhythmic foundation by using different rhythmic patterns and variations to create interest and variation in the song. Experiment with different drum beats, time signatures, and tempo changes to create a dynamic and engaging rhythm.

Use contrast and variation: Create contrast and variation by incorporating different elements into the song. Experiment with dynamics, instrumentation, arrangement, and production to create interest and variation throughout the song.

Collaborate with others: Collaborate with other songwriters, musicians, and producers to gain new perspectives and ideas. Collaborating can help you break out of your creative comfort zone and explore new ways of incorporating melody, harmony, rhythm, and lyrics into your songwriting process.

Practice, practice, practice: Songwriting, like any skill, requires practice and dedication. Set aside time each day to work on your songwriting skills, experiment with different techniques, and develop your own unique style.

In conclusion, incorporating melody, harmony, rhythm, and lyrics into songwriting requires skill, practice, and experimentation. By using these techniques, songwriters can create cohesive and compelling pieces of music that connect with audiences on a deeper level. Remember to stay true to your own unique style and to collaborate with others to gain new perspectives and ideas. With practice and dedication, you can become a successful songwriter and create music that stands the test of time.

# CHAPTER 3
# FINDING INSPIRATION FOR SONGWRITING

## STRATEGIES FOR FINDING INSPIRATION FOR SONGWRITING

Songwriting can be a challenging and sometimes daunting task. Finding inspiration is crucial in creating songs that are unique, memorable, and relatable. In this section, we will explore strategies for finding inspiration for songwriting, including personal experiences, emotions, and current events.

Draw from personal experiences: Personal experiences are a great source of inspiration for songwriting. Think about the people, places, and events that have had a significant impact on your life. These experiences can be used to create lyrics that are relatable and meaningful to your audience.

Tap into your emotions: Emotions can be a powerful source of inspiration for songwriting. Whether it's love, heartbreak, anger, or happiness, emotions can be used to create lyrics that evoke a strong emotional response from your audience. Try to be vulnerable and honest with your emotions, as this can help create more authentic and relatable songs.

Use current events: Current events can be a great source of inspiration for songwriting. Think about the news stories and issues that are affecting people around the world. Use these events as a starting point to create lyrics that address important social and political issues.

Find inspiration in literature and poetry: Literature and poetry can provide inspiration for songwriting. Read books, poems, and other literary works that resonate with you. Use the language, imagery, and themes from these works to create lyrics that are creative and unique.

Collaborate with others: Collaborating with other songwriters, musicians, and producers can help spark new ideas and inspiration. Working with others can also help you break out of your creative comfort zone and explore new styles and genres.

Experiment with different styles and genres: Experimenting with different styles and genres can help you find inspiration and develop your own unique style. Listen to music from different genres and cultures, and incorporate elements from these styles into your own songwriting.

Take a break: Sometimes, the best way to find inspiration is to take a break from songwriting. Take a walk, read a book, or do something else that inspires you. Taking a break can help clear your mind and provide fresh perspective when you return to your songwriting.

In conclusion, finding inspiration for songwriting can be a challenging task, but there are many strategies that can be used to spark creativity and develop unique ideas. Drawing from personal experiences, emotions, and current events, as well as collaborating with others, experimenting with different styles and genres, and taking a break, are all effective ways to find inspiration for songwriting. Remember to stay true to your own unique style and to be open to new ideas and perspectives. With practice and dedication, you can become a successful songwriter and create music that resonates with audiences around the world.

# TECHNIQUES FOR DEVELOPING THEMES AND CONCEPTS FOR SONGS

Developing themes and concepts for songs can be a challenging task. However, with the right techniques, it is possible to develop ideas and create songs that are meaningful and resonant with audiences. Here are some techniques for developing themes and concepts for songs:

Finding inspiration in your environment: Look around you for inspiration. Think about your surroundings, your relationships, and your experiences. Consider the people, places, and events that have impacted you, and how you can use these as themes or concepts in your songs.

Exploring emotions: Emotions are a powerful source of inspiration for songwriting. Consider the emotions you have experienced, and how you can express them through lyrics and melodies. Think about how you want your audience to feel when they listen to your song, and how you can use emotions to create that effect.

Using metaphor and symbolism: Metaphors and symbolism can be used to create deeper meaning in your songs. Think about how you can use metaphors and symbols to represent your themes and concepts. For example, using a tree as a metaphor for personal growth, or a river as a symbol for the passage of time.

Collaborating with others: Collaborating with other songwriters, musicians, and producers can help you develop themes and concepts for your songs. Working with others can also help you break out of your creative comfort zone and explore new ideas and perspectives.

Brainstorming: Brainstorming is a classic technique used in many creative processes, including songwriting. Simply start by writing down anything that comes to mind. Don't worry about grammar or whether an idea seems silly or irrelevant. The goal is to generate a large number of ideas quickly. Once you have a list of potential themes and concepts, you can begin to refine and develop them further.

Telling a story: Stories are a great way to engage your audience and create a narrative for your song. Think about a story you want to tell and how you can use it as a basis for your theme or concept. Consider the characters, setting, and conflict, and how you can use these elements to create a powerful and engaging song.

Experimenting with different styles and genres: Experimenting with different styles and genres can help you find inspiration and develop your own unique style. Try writing songs in different genres or using different instruments. This can help you discover new themes and concepts that you may not have considered before.

In conclusion, developing themes and concepts for songs can be a challenging task, but with the right techniques, it is possible to create meaningful and resonant music. Brainstorming, finding inspiration in your environment, exploring emotions, using metaphor and symbolism, telling a story, collaborating with others, and experimenting with different styles and genres are all effective techniques for developing themes and concepts for songs. Remember to stay true to your own unique style and to be open to new ideas and perspectives. With practice and dedication, you can become a successful songwriter and create music that resonates with audiences around the world.

# STRATEGIES FOR OVERCOMING WRITER'S BLOCK AND OTHER CREATIVE OBSTACLES

Writer's block and other creative obstacles are common challenges that songwriters face. However, with the right strategies, it is possible to overcome these obstacles and keep the creative process flowing. Here are some strategies for overcoming writer's block and other creative obstacles:

Take a break: Sometimes, the best thing to do when you are feeling stuck is to step away from your work. Take a break and engage in other activities that you enjoy. This can help clear your mind and provide new inspiration for your songwriting.

Change your environment: A change of scenery can be helpful when you are feeling uninspired. Consider taking your work to a new location, such as a park, coffee shop, or library. This can help you break out of your routine and stimulate your creativity.

Collaborate with others: Collaborating with other songwriters, musicians, or producers can help you break out of your creative rut and provide new ideas and perspectives. Working with others can also help you stay motivated and accountable.

Practice mindfulness: Mindfulness techniques, such as meditation or yoga, can help you clear your mind and reduce stress and anxiety. This can help you focus on your creative process and overcome creative blocks.

Try a different approach: If you are struggling to write lyrics, try writing melodies instead. If you are stuck on a particular section of a song, try working on a different section. Sometimes, a change in approach can help you see your work in a new light and provide new inspiration.

Set deadlines and goals: Setting deadlines and goals for your songwriting can help keep you motivated and focused. This can also help you overcome procrastination and get back on track when you are feeling stuck.

Keep practicing: Practice is essential for improving your songwriting skills and overcoming creative obstacles. Keep writing, even if you feel like your work is not at the level you want it to be. The more you practice, the more you will improve.

In conclusion, writer's block and other creative obstacles are common challenges that songwriters face. However, with the right strategies, it is possible to overcome these obstacles and keep the creative process flowing. Taking a break, changing your environment, collaborating with others, practicing mindfulness, trying a different approach, setting deadlines and goals, and keeping practicing are all effective strategies for overcoming writer's block and other creative obstacles. Remember to be patient with yourself and to stay committed to your craft. With dedication and perseverance, you can overcome any creative obstacle and create music that resonates with audiences around the world.

# CHAPTER 4

# DEVELOPING SONG STRUCTURE

## A REVIEW OF POPULAR SONG STRUCTURES

Song structure is a crucial aspect of songwriting, as it can significantly impact the overall flow, emotional impact, and reception of a song. Choosing the right structure can be influenced by several factors, including the genre, target audience, and desired emotional response. In this section, we will explore some of the most popular song structures, highlighting their unique features and benefits.

### Verse-Chorus Structure

The verse-chorus structure is the most commonly used song structure in popular music, and it has stood the test of time for a good reason. This structure consists of alternating verses and choruses, where the verses typically provide the narrative or description of a situation, and the choruses contain the hook or message of the song.

One of the key advantages of this structure is its simplicity. It is easy for listeners to follow along and sing along to, which can contribute to the song's popularity and success. Another advantage is its flexibility, which allows songwriters to vary the melody, lyrics, and chords of each section to create different emotions and moods. However, one potential disadvantage is that the repetitive nature of the structure can become predictable, making the song less engaging or interesting to some listeners.

## AABA Structure

The AABA structure is commonly used in jazz and blues music, consisting of four sections, where the first two sections have the same melody and lyrics (A), followed by a contrasting section (B), and then a return to the original melody and lyrics (A). This structure is effective in creating songs with a clear sense of narrative and progression. The contrast between the A and B sections creates tension and release.

One of the benefits of this structure is its flexibility, allowing variations in the melody and lyrics of each section. It also permits extended improvisation in the B section, which can showcase the performer's skills and creativity. However, one potential drawback is that the structure may be less accessible to some listeners, who may find the repetition of the A section less engaging.

## Verse-Prechorus-Chorus Structure

The verse-prechorus-chorus structure is a variation of the verse-chorus structure, with an additional prechorus section placed between the verse and chorus. The prechorus serves to build up tension and anticipation, leading to the chorus, which is the most memorable and catchy part of the song. This structure is effective in creating songs that gradually build in intensity and excitement as the prechorus serves as a bridge between the verse and chorus.

One of the significant advantages of this structure is its ability to create a dynamic and engaging song, with a clear sense of progression and climax. The prechorus can also provide a contrast to the verse, either melodically or lyrically, making the chorus more impactful. However, one potential disadvantage is that the prechorus can become repetitive or predictable, depending on the melody and lyrics.

# ABABCB Structure

The ABABCB structure, also known as the pop song form, is a variation of the verse-chorus structure that includes an additional bridge section placed between the second chorus and final chorus. The bridge provides a contrast to the rest of the song, either melodically or lyrically, creating a sense of release and resolution. This structure is effective in creating songs with a strong sense of progression and development, as the bridge serves as a climax to the song.

One of the benefits of this structure is its ability to create a memorable and engaging song, with a clear sense of development and climax. The bridge can also provide an opportunity for experimentation and creativity, as it allows for a departure from the main melody and structure of the song. However, one potential disadvantage is that the structure can become predictable or formulaic, depending on how the song is executed.

# AAA Structure

AAA structure is a simple yet effective song structure that consists of three identical sections. This structure is often used in folk and traditional music, as well as some contemporary songs. The repetition of the same section creates a sense of familiarity and comfort, making it easy for listeners to sing along.

One of the benefits of this structure is its simplicity, as it allows the focus to be on the melody, lyrics, and emotional impact of the song. The repetition of the same section also provides a sense of unity and coherence, making the song feel like a complete whole. However, one potential disadvantage is that the lack of variation can make the song less engaging or interesting to some listeners.

In conclusion, there is no one-size-fits-all approach to song structure, as it depends on various factors such as genre, target audience, and desired emotional response. However, understanding the different structures and their unique features can help songwriters make more informed decisions when crafting their songs. Ultimately, the most important factor is the emotional impact of the song, and a well-crafted structure can contribute to that impact by creating a sense of progression, tension, and release.

# TECHNIQUES FOR DEVELOPING AND ORGANIZING SONG STRUCTURE

Developing and organizing a song structure can be a challenging task, especially for new songwriters. However, there are some techniques that can help simplify the process and make it more manageable.

Start with the chorus: Some songwriters prefer to start with the chorus because it is the most memorable and recognizable part of the song. Once you have a solid chorus, you can build the rest of the song around it.

Use a pre-existing structure: As mentioned earlier, there are many popular song structures that you can use as a starting point. For example, you could start with a simple verse-chorus-verse structure and then add a bridge or pre-chorus to create more variation.

Experiment with different structures: While it can be helpful to start with a pre-existing structure, don't be afraid to experiment with different structures or even create your own. For example, you could try a verse-verse-chorus-verse structure or a chorus-verse-chorus-bridge-chorus structure.

Consider the emotional impact: As you develop your structure, think about the emotional impact you want to create. For example, if you want to build tension and suspense, you might use a verse-chorus-verse-chorus-bridge structure, where the bridge provides a release from the tension.

Use repetition and variation: Repetition can create a sense of familiarity and comfort, but too much repetition can make the song boring. Try to balance repetition with variation to keep the song interesting and engaging.

Pay attention to transitions: The transitions between sections can be just as important as the sections themselves. Smooth transitions can help create a sense of flow and continuity, while abrupt transitions can create a sense of surprise or contrast.

Edit and revise: Finally, remember that songwriting is a process, and it may take several drafts to get the structure just right. Don't be afraid to edit and revise as needed to create the best possible structure for your song.

# STRATEGIES FOR CREATING MEMORABLE HOOKS AND MELODIES

Hooks and melodies are the backbone of many successful songs, and creating a memorable melody that captivates the listener is an important part of the songwriting process. Here are some strategies and techniques for creating hooks and melodies that stick in the listener's mind.

Start with a catchy phrase: A good hook usually starts with a catchy phrase or melody that is easy to remember. It can be a simple phrase or a series of notes that are repeated throughout the song.

Keep it simple: Simple melodies are often the most memorable, as they are easier to sing and remember. Try to keep your melodies simple and repetitive, with a catchy and memorable hook that listeners can sing along with.

Experiment with rhythm: Rhythm can be an effective way to make a melody more memorable. Try experimenting with different rhythms, syncopation, and accents to create a unique and catchy melody.

Use repetition: Repetition is a powerful tool for making a melody stick in the listener's mind. Repeat key phrases or words throughout the song, or use repetition to create a pattern that the listener can follow.

Use contrasting sections: Contrast can make a melody more interesting and memorable. Try to create contrasting sections within your melody, such as a high-pitched chorus followed by a low-pitched verse, or a slow and gentle verse followed by a fast and upbeat chorus.

Use familiar scales: Familiar scales, such as major and minor scales, are often used in popular music because they are familiar to listeners and easy to sing. Try experimenting with different scales to create unique and memorable melodies.

Use unexpected intervals: Intervals are the distance between two notes, and using unexpected intervals can make a melody more interesting and memorable. Try using unexpected intervals within your melody to create tension and surprise.

Collaborate with others: Collaboration can also be helpful when creating hooks and melodies. Working with other songwriters or musicians can bring new ideas and perspectives to the table, and help you create a more memorable melody.

Remember, creating a memorable melody takes time and practice. Don't be afraid to experiment and try new things, and be willing to revise and refine your ideas until you find something that truly sticks in the listener's mind. In addition to these techniques, it's important to consider the overall structure and theme of the song when creating a melody. The melody should fit the lyrics and complement the overall mood and message of the song.

Ultimately, the most important thing when creating a melody is to trust your instincts and follow your creative impulses. Don't be afraid to take risks and try something new, and remember that the best melodies often come from unexpected places. With practice and perseverance, you can create hooks and melodies that capture the listener's attention and keep them coming back for more.

# CHAPTER 5

# WRITING EFFECTIVE LYRICS

## STRATEGIES FOR WRITING LYRICS THAT ARE MEMORABLE, MEANINGFUL, AND CONNECT WITH AUDIENCES

Lyrics are a crucial part of any song, as they convey the message and emotion of the song to the listener. Writing lyrics that are memorable, meaningful, and connect with audiences is an art form that requires both creativity and technique. Here are some strategies and techniques for writing lyrics that resonate with listeners.

Start with a strong concept: A strong concept is the foundation of any great song. Start by brainstorming ideas and concepts that are meaningful to you, and that you think will resonate with your audience. Once you have a strong concept, you can build your lyrics around it.

Use concrete details: Concrete details help to bring a song to life, and make it more relatable to listeners. Use specific and descriptive language to paint a picture in the listener's mind, and help them connect with the emotion and message of the song.

Write from personal experience: Writing from personal experience is a powerful way to connect with listeners, as it adds authenticity and emotion to your lyrics. Draw on your own experiences and emotions to create lyrics that are heartfelt and meaningful.

Use metaphor and imagery: Metaphors and imagery are powerful tools for creating vivid and memorable lyrics. Use metaphors and imagery to convey complex emotions and ideas in a way that is easy for listeners to understand.

Consider the melody: The melody of a song also influences the lyrics. Consider the mood and tone of the melody, and let it guide your lyrics. Use the melody to convey the emotion and message of the song, and to create a strong connection between the lyrics and the music.

Edit and revise: Writing great lyrics takes time and effort, and it's important to be willing to edit and revise your work until you get it right. Take the time to review your lyrics, and be willing to make changes and adjustments as needed to create lyrics that are truly memorable and meaningful.

Collaborate with others: Collaboration can also be helpful when writing lyrics. Working with other songwriters or musicians can bring new ideas and perspectives to the table, and help you create lyrics that connect with your audience.

Use social media and other platforms for feedback: Sharing your lyrics on social media or other platforms can be a great way to get feedback from your audience. Use feedback from listeners to refine and improve your lyrics, and to create lyrics that truly connect with your audience.

Remember, writing great lyrics takes practice and perseverance. Don't be afraid to experiment and try new things, and be willing to revise and refine your work until you get it right. By using these strategies and techniques, you can create lyrics that are both memorable and meaningful, and that connect with audiences on a deep and emotional level.

# TECHNIQUES FOR USING RHYME, IMAGERY, AND OTHER LITERARY DEVICES IN LYRICS

Lyrics are an important part of any song, and using literary devices can help to make them more engaging and memorable for listeners. Here are some techniques for using rhyme, imagery, and other literary devices in your lyrics.

Rhyme: Rhyme is one of the most common and effective techniques for making lyrics memorable. Rhyming words create a sense of musicality and rhythm in the lyrics, and can help to make them catchier and more memorable. There are different types of rhyme, including end rhyme (where the last syllables of two or more lines rhyme), internal rhyme (where rhyming words appear within the same line), and slant rhyme (where the rhyming words have similar but not identical sounds).

Imagery: Imagery is another powerful technique for making lyrics more engaging and memorable. By using vivid and descriptive language, you can create a mental picture in the listener's mind, and help them to connect with the emotion and message of the song. Imagery can be used to describe people, places, and things, and can help to create a sense of atmosphere and mood in the song.

Metaphors and similes: Metaphors and similes are two other common literary devices used in song lyrics. Metaphors involve making a comparison between two things that are not alike, in order to create a deeper meaning or understanding. Similes are similar, but involve using the words "like" or "as" to make the comparison more explicit. Both techniques can be used to create a sense of depth and complexity in the lyrics, and to help listeners connect with the emotion and message of the song.

Personification: Personification involves giving human qualities to non-human things, such as animals, objects, or abstract concepts. This technique can be used to make the lyrics more relatable and engaging for listeners, and to create a sense of empathy and emotion in the song.

Alliteration and consonance: Alliteration involves using the same consonant sound at the beginning of multiple words in a line, while consonance involves using the same consonant sound within a line. Both techniques can be used to create a sense of rhythm and musicality in the lyrics, and to make them more memorable for listeners.

Repetition: Repetition involves repeating words or phrases throughout the song, and can be used to create a sense of emphasis or urgency. Repetition can also help to make the lyrics more memorable, and to create a strong connection between the lyrics and the

Experimentation: Finally, it's important to be willing to experiment and try new things when using literary devices in your lyrics. Don't be afraid to take risks and push boundaries, and be open to feedback and critique from other songwriters or musicians. By being creative and innovative with your use of literary devices, you can create lyrics that are truly unique and memorable.

In conclusion, using literary devices can be an effective way to make your lyrics more engaging and memorable for listeners. By incorporating techniques such as rhyme, imagery, metaphors, and repetition, you can create lyrics that are both meaningful and catchy, and that connect with your audience on a deep and emotional level.

# TIPS FOR BALANCING FORM AND CONTENT IN LYRICS

The art of songwriting is all about finding the right balance between form and content in lyrics. While it's important to have a strong structure and catchy melody, lyrics are the heart and soul of a song. They convey the emotions, message, and story that the songwriter wants to share with their audience. As such, finding the right words and phrases to express these elements can be one of the most challenging aspects of the songwriting process.

To strike the right balance between form and content, there are several tips that songwriters can follow:

Start with a clear idea: Before you even begin to write your lyrics, it's important to have a clear idea of what you want to express. This could be a specific emotion, story, or message. Having a clear idea in mind can help guide your writing and ensure that you stay focused on the content of your lyrics.

Use concrete details: To make your lyrics more meaningful and memorable, it's important to use concrete details and imagery. Rather than relying on abstract concepts or generalizations, try to describe specific images, sounds, and emotions that will help your listeners connect with your song on a deeper level.

Avoid clichés: While it can be tempting to use clichés and familiar phrases in your lyrics, doing so can make your song feel generic and unoriginal. Instead, try to come up with fresh, original ways to express your ideas.

Experiment with structure: While most songs follow a specific structure, such as verse-chorus-verse-chorus-bridge-chorus, there's no rule that says you have to stick to this format. Experimenting with different structures, such as starting with the chorus or using a different number of verses, can help make your song stand out and keep your listeners engaged.

Edit ruthlessly: Once you've written your lyrics, it's important to edit and revise them carefully. This may mean cutting out lines or even entire verses that don't contribute to the overall message or feeling of the song. By editing ruthlessly, you can ensure that your lyrics are focused, meaningful, and impactful.

Collaborate with others: Sometimes, working with other songwriters or musicians can help you strike the right balance between form and content. By bouncing ideas off of each other and getting feedback from others, you can refine your lyrics and ensure that they resonate with your audience.

Don't be afraid to be vulnerable: Some of the most powerful songs are those that come from a place of vulnerability and honesty. Don't be afraid to share your own personal experiences and emotions in your lyrics, even if they feel uncomfortable or difficult to express. By doing so, you can create a deeper connection with your audience and make your song more meaningful and memorable.

# CHAPTER 6
# COLLABORATIVE SONGWRITING

## THE BENEFITS AND CHALLENGES OF COLLABORATIVE SONGWRITING

Collaborative songwriting is a process where two or more songwriters work together to create a piece of music. The process can involve sharing ideas, melodies, and lyrics, and working together to refine them into a cohesive whole. Collaborative songwriting can be incredibly rewarding, but it also comes with its own unique benefits and challenges.

One of the main benefits of collaborative songwriting is that it allows for a broader range of ideas and perspectives to be incorporated into the song. When working with other songwriters, you can bounce ideas off each other, inspire each other, and draw on each other's strengths to create a piece of music that is greater than the sum of its parts. Collaborating with other musicians and songwriters can also help you to learn new techniques and approaches to songwriting, which can help you to grow as an artist.

Another benefit of collaborative songwriting is that it can help to alleviate some of the pressure that comes with writing a song on your own. Songwriting can be a solitary and challenging process, and working with others can make it feel less daunting. Collaborating with other songwriters can also help to keep you motivated and focused, as you work towards a shared goal.

However, collaborative songwriting also comes with its own challenges. One of the main challenges is finding the right people to work with. Collaborative songwriting requires a certain level of trust, communication, and compatibility, and finding songwriters who share your creative vision and work ethic can be difficult. There is also the risk that creative differences can arise during the songwriting process, which can lead to tension and conflict.

Another challenge of collaborative songwriting is that it requires compromise. When working with other songwriters, you may need to make concessions and sacrifices in order to ensure that everyone's ideas are represented. This can be difficult, particularly if you feel strongly about a particular aspect of the song.

In conclusion, collaborative songwriting can be a rewarding and inspiring process that can lead to some of the most memorable songs in music history. However, it requires finding the right collaborators, effective communication, compromise, and an open-minded approach to creative ideas. By embracing the benefits and challenges of collaborative songwriting, songwriters can create music that truly reflects their creative vision and resonates with their audiences.

# STRATEGIES FOR FINDING AND WORKING WITH COLLABORATORS

Finding and working with collaborators is an important aspect of collaborative songwriting. It requires a certain level of trust, communication, and compatibility, and finding songwriters who share your creative vision and work ethic can be challenging. However, there are several strategies that can help you to find and work effectively with collaborators.

Use Online Platforms: There are several online platforms that connect songwriters and musicians with one another. These platforms allow you to search for collaborators based on specific criteria, such as location, genre, and skill level. Some popular platforms include SoundBetter, BandMix, and SongwriterLink.

Collaborate with Musicians You Know: Collaborating with musicians you already know and trust can be an effective way to get started with collaborative songwriting. You can reach out to friends, acquaintances, or musicians you have worked with in the past and see if they are interested in working on a project with you.

Be Open-Minded: When working with collaborators, it's important to be open-minded and willing to listen to different ideas and perspectives. Collaborative songwriting requires compromise and a willingness to work together to achieve a shared goal. It's important to communicate openly and respectfully with your collaborators, and to be willing to make concessions and compromises when necessary.

Establish Clear Roles and Expectations: When working with collaborators, it's important to establish clear roles and expectations upfront. This can help to prevent misunderstandings and ensure that everyone is on the same page. You should discuss who will be responsible for each aspect of the songwriting process, such as writing lyrics, creating melodies, and arranging the music.

Communicate Effectively: Effective communication is essential when working with collaborators. You should establish a clear system for communicating ideas and feedback, and be open to receiving constructive criticism from your collaborators. It's also important to be responsive and respectful in your communication, and to avoid any confrontational or negative language.

In conclusion, finding and working with collaborators is a key aspect of collaborative songwriting. By attending workshops and events, using online platforms, collaborating with musicians you already know, being open-minded, establishing clear roles and expectations, and communicating effectively, you can find and work effectively with collaborators who share your creative vision and help you to create great music.

## TECHNIQUES FOR NAVIGATING CREATIVE DIFFERENCES AND BUILDING STRONG CREATIVE PARTNERSHIPS

Collaborative songwriting can be a rewarding and exciting process, but it can also be challenging at times. Creative differences can arise, and it's important to be able to navigate these differences and build strong creative partnerships. Here are some techniques for doing so:

Listen to Each Other: One of the most important aspects of building a strong creative partnership is to listen to each other. It's important to be open to your collaborator's ideas and perspectives, and to show respect for their creative contributions. By actively listening and valuing each other's input, you can build a stronger, more collaborative creative partnership.

Communicate Effectively: Effective communication is essential for navigating creative differences and building strong partnerships. You should establish a clear system for communicating ideas and feedback, and be open to receiving constructive criticism from your collaborator. It's also important to be responsive and respectful in your communication, and to avoid any confrontational or negative language.

Be Flexible: It's important to be flexible and willing to compromise when working with collaborators. Everyone has their own creative vision, and it's important to find a way to blend those visions together to create something that is greater than the sum of its parts. This may require making concessions and compromises, but the end result will be a stronger and more cohesive song.

Establish Clear Roles and Expectations: When working with collaborators, it's important to establish clear roles and expectations upfront. This can help to prevent misunderstandings and ensure that everyone is on the same page. You should discuss who will be responsible for each aspect of the songwriting process, such as writing lyrics, creating melodies, and arranging the music.

Embrace Creative Differences: Creative differences can be challenging, but they can also be an opportunity for growth and innovation. By embracing your collaborator's different perspectives and ideas, you can create something that is truly unique and original. Remember that creative partnerships are about finding a way to blend different creative visions together, and that the end result will be stronger for it.

Celebrate Successes: Finally, it's important to celebrate successes and milestones along the way. Collaborative songwriting can be a long and sometimes difficult process, but it's important to acknowledge and celebrate the successes along the way. This can help to build morale and strengthen your creative partnership.

In conclusion, navigating creative differences and building strong creative partnerships is essential for successful collaborative songwriting. By listening to each other, communicating effectively, being flexible, establishing clear roles and expectations, embracing creative differences, and celebrating successes, you can build a strong and successful creative partnership that produces great music.

# CHAPTER 7
# CRAFTING HIT SONGS

## THE CHARACTERISTICS OF SUCCESSFUL HIT SONGS

Successful hit songs share several common characteristics that contribute to their popularity and appeal. These songs stand out from the rest and capture the hearts of millions of fans worldwide.

One of the primary features of a hit song is a catchy and memorable hook that grabs the listener's attention and stays in their head long after the song has ended. A hook is a short, repeating melody or phrase that serves as the song's centerpiece, and it can be found in the chorus, the verse, or even in the instrumental sections of the song. A good hook should be easy to sing along to and have a simple, catchy melody that sticks with the listener. Hooks are so essential that they often determine the success or failure of a song.

Another important characteristic of hit songs is their relatable lyrics. Successful songwriters often write about universal themes and experiences that many people can identify with, such as love, heartbreak, and personal growth. They use vivid imagery and poetic language to convey their message, creating a sense of emotional connection between the listener and the song. The lyrics should be easy to understand, yet deep enough to convey a message that resonates with listeners.

Strong melodies are also key to the success of hit songs. A melody is the sequence of notes that form the song's main musical line, and it should be memorable, singable, and pleasing to the ear. Successful songwriters spend a lot of time crafting and perfecting the melody, experimenting with different chord progressions and note arrangements to create something unique and memorable. A strong melody is one that can be instantly recognized by the listener and easily recalled even after a long time has passed.

The structure of the song is also crucial in creating a hit. There are different structures that songwriters can use, such as verse-chorus, AABA, and others. Regardless of the structure used, the song's structure must be coherent and flow smoothly. The verse and chorus should work together to create a cohesive and memorable musical experience for the listener. A good song structure should keep the listener engaged from beginning to end.

Successful songwriters often use literary devices, such as rhyme and imagery, to enhance the lyrics and create a more memorable experience for the listener. Rhyme is the repetition of sounds in two or more words, often at the end of a line, and it can help create a more cohesive and memorable lyrical experience. Imagery is the use of descriptive language to paint a picture in the listener's mind and make the lyrics more relatable.

Balancing form and content is also a crucial aspect of successful songwriting. The content of the song should match the form and structure, and it should be concise and focused. The lyrics should be written with the melody and rhythm in mind, and they should fit seamlessly with the musical composition. Successful songwriters know how to balance the form and content to create a song that is both memorable and meaningful.

Collaborative songwriting is another way that successful songwriters create hit songs. Working with other musicians and songwriters can bring new ideas and perspectives to the creative process, leading to more innovative and successful songs. However, collaboration can also be challenging, and it requires strong communication and creative skills to navigate differences in style and opinion.

In conclusion, successful hit songs share several key characteristics, including a catchy hook, relatable lyrics, strong melodies, and a coherent song structure. Songwriters who can balance form and content, use literary devices effectively, and collaborate with others can create memorable and meaningful songs that connect with audiences worldwide.

# STRATEGIES FOR MARKETING AND PROMOTING SONGS

Writing a hit song is just the beginning of the journey towards success in the music industry. Once a song is written, it needs to be marketed and promoted to reach the widest possible audience. There are numerous strategies that songwriters can use to promote their work, build their brand, and connect with fans.

One of the most important strategies for promoting a song is to use social media platforms to build an online presence. This can include creating a website, a YouTube channel, or a social media account on platforms such as Facebook, Twitter, and Instagram. By sharing music, behind-the-scenes footage, and other engaging content on these platforms, songwriters can connect with fans and build a following.

Another important strategy for promoting a song is to leverage the power of streaming platforms such as Spotify and Apple Music. These platforms have become the dominant way that people listen to music, and getting a song onto a popular playlist can lead to a huge boost in exposure. Songwriters can also use targeted advertising on these platforms to reach new listeners.

Live performances are another crucial way for songwriters to promote their work. Playing shows and festivals can help to build a following, connect with fans, and generate buzz around a new song. In addition to traditional live performances, songwriters can also use virtual events such as live streaming concerts to reach audiences around the world.

Collaborating with other artists and influencers is another effective way to promote a song. By working with other musicians, songwriters can tap into their audiences and build new connections. Collaborating with influencers such as YouTubers, bloggers, and social media personalities can also help to increase exposure and build a following.

In addition to these strategies, there are a number of other marketing techniques that songwriters can use to promote their work. These can include reaching out to music bloggers and journalists, creating merchandise and other promotional materials, and using email marketing and other direct outreach techniques to connect with fans.

Of course, promoting a song can be a challenging and time-consuming process, and success is never guaranteed. However, by using a combination of these strategies and staying persistent and focused, songwriters can increase their chances of reaching a wider audience and achieving success in the music industry.

# TECHNIQUES FOR BUILDING A SUCCESSFUL CAREER AS A SONGWRITER

Songwriting is a highly competitive field, and building a successful career as a songwriter can be challenging. However, with the right strategies and techniques, it is possible to make a name for yourself and achieve success as a songwriter.

One of the most important things you can do to build a successful career as a songwriter is to network. Attend industry events, connect with other songwriters, and work to build relationships with music industry professionals such as producers, publishers, and A&R executives. These connections can help you get your foot in the door and can lead to opportunities for collaboration and exposure.

Another important aspect of building a successful songwriting career is to stay up-to-date with industry trends and developments. Keep an eye on what's happening in the music industry, stay on top of emerging genres and artists, and make sure you are familiar with the latest technologies and platforms that are being used to distribute and promote music.

It's also important to be persistent and determined. Building a successful songwriting career takes time, and you will likely encounter setbacks and obstacles along the way. However, if you are passionate about your craft and committed to your goals, you can overcome these challenges and achieve success.

In addition to these strategies, there are a number of techniques you can use to build a successful career as a songwriter. One important technique is to focus on writing for specific markets and artists. Identify the types of songs that are most popular with particular artists or within certain genres, and work to craft songs that fit those criteria. This can increase your chances of getting your songs heard by the right people and can help you build a reputation as a songwriter who understands the needs of the industry.

Another technique is to be proactive in promoting your work. Take advantage of social media platforms like Facebook, Twitter, and Instagram to share your music and connect with fans and industry professionals. Consider creating a website to showcase your work and make it easy for people to find and listen to your songs.

Finally, it's important to stay true to your artistic vision and to never stop honing your craft. Continuously work to improve your songwriting skills, experiment with new techniques and approaches, and stay open to feedback and constructive criticism. By staying focused and committed, and by continually striving to grow and improve as a songwriter, you can build a successful career in this exciting and rewarding field.

# CHAPTER 8
# CONCLUSION

## SUMMARY OF THE KEY POINTS IN THE BOOK

In this book, "The Art of Songwriting: Techniques and Strategies for Creating Hit Songs," we explored the world of songwriting and the key elements that contribute to creating successful, memorable songs.

We began by discussing the importance of songwriting in the music industry and how it differs from other musical skills. We then explored the challenges and rewards of successful songwriting, including the importance of creativity, discipline, and perseverance.

The basic elements of songwriting were then reviewed, including melody, harmony, rhythm, and lyrics, and we discussed the importance of each element in creating successful songs. We provided techniques for incorporating these elements into songwriting and strategies for finding inspiration, developing themes and concepts, and overcoming creative obstacles.

We then delved into popular song structures, such as verse-chorus, AABA, and other forms, and provided techniques for developing and organizing song structure, as well as strategies for creating memorable hooks and melodies.

We then focused on the art of writing lyrics, discussing techniques for using rhyme, imagery, and other literary devices, and providing tips for balancing form and content in lyrics. We also discussed the benefits and challenges of collaborative songwriting, and provided strategies for finding and working with collaborators, as well as techniques for navigating creative differences and building strong partnerships.

Finally, we explored the characteristics of successful hit songs, including catchy hooks, relatable lyrics, and strong melodies. We provided strategies for marketing and promoting songs, as well as techniques for building a successful career as a songwriter.

In summary, this book provides a comprehensive guide to the art of songwriting, covering all aspects of the process from inspiration to marketing. It is a must-read for anyone interested in pursuing a career in songwriting or simply looking to improve their songwriting skills.

# REFLECTION ON THE ONGOING IMPORTANCE OF SONGWRITING IN THE MUSIC INDUSTRY AND SOCIETY

The ongoing importance of songwriting in the music industry and society cannot be overstated. Throughout history, songs have played a vital role in human culture, from folk songs that have been passed down through generations to contemporary hits that dominate the charts.

At its core, songwriting is about communication. It is a means for artists to express their ideas, emotions, and experiences to audiences in a way that resonates with them. Songs can tell stories, evoke powerful emotions, and create a sense of connection between artists and listeners.

In today's music industry, songwriting is more important than ever. The rise of digital platforms and the democratization of music production means that anyone can create and release music. This has resulted in an incredibly crowded and competitive marketplace, where the quality of the songwriting has become a crucial factor in determining an artist's success. The best songs are those that can cut through the noise and capture the attention of audiences, building a dedicated fanbase and establishing an artist's career.

Furthermore, songwriting has the power to address important social and political issues, and can be a platform for artists to express their views and advocate for change. From Bob Dylan's iconic protest songs of the 1960s to contemporary artists like Kendrick Lamar and Billie Eilish who tackle issues such as social inequality and mental health, songwriting can have a profound impact on society. It can bring people together and serve as a unifying force, helping to bridge divides and create a sense of community.

Beyond its cultural and social impact, songwriting is also a valuable skill for musicians and songwriters looking to build a career in the music industry. The ability to write strong and memorable songs can help artists stand out from the competition and attract the attention of industry professionals. Songwriting royalties can also provide a significant source of income for songwriters, even after the song's initial release.

In conclusion, the ongoing importance of songwriting cannot be underestimated. It is a powerful form of expression that has the ability to inspire, connect, and create change. Whether you are a seasoned songwriter or just starting out, honing your songwriting skills can help you build a successful career in the music industry and make a meaningful impact on society.

# FINAL THOUGHTS

Songwriting is truly an art form that requires a unique combination of creativity, skill, and perseverance. In this book, we have explored the key elements of successful songwriting, including melody, harmony, rhythm, and lyrics, as well as the importance of themes, concepts, and song structure. We have also discussed strategies for finding inspiration, overcoming writer's block, and working collaboratively.

However, while the technical aspects of songwriting are important, it is ultimately the emotional impact of a song that connects with audiences and creates lasting cultural significance. Successful songwriters are not just skilled musicians, but also empathetic storytellers who can capture the essence of the human experience in a way that resonates with others.

Moreover, songwriting is not just a personal passion, but also a viable career path in the music industry. In today's digital age, the opportunities for songwriters to reach new audiences and build successful careers are more accessible than ever before. With dedication, persistence, and a willingness to learn and adapt, aspiring songwriters can make a name for themselves and leave their mark on the world.

In conclusion, the art of songwriting is an ever-evolving craft that continues to shape the music industry and inspire generations. By studying the techniques and strategies outlined in this book, aspiring songwriters can hone their skills and become part of this rich and vibrant tradition. Whether for personal expression or professional success, the art of songwriting has the power to transform both the individual and the world around them.

Printed in Great Britain
by Amazon

21464757R00032